Deep Field

Mari Bolte

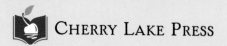
CHERRY LAKE PRESS

Published in the United States of America by Cherry Lake Publishing Group
Ann Arbor, Michigan
www.cherrylakepublishing.com

Reading Adviser: Beth Walker Gambro, MS, Ed., Reading Consultant, Yorkville, IL
Content Adviser: Robert S. Kowalczyk, MS, Physics, Systems Engineer (Retired) at the NASA Jet Propulsion Laboratory

Photo Credits: page 1: ©NASA, ESA, CSA, STSCI, Webb Ero Production Team/nasa.gov; page 5: ©Rogelio Bernal Andreo/nasa.gov; page 6: ©Artur Debat/Getty Images; page 9: ©sololos/Getty Images; page 10: ©NASA, ESA, CSA, and STScI/flickr.com; page 13: ©NASA, ESA, B. Welch (JHU), D. Coe (STScI), A. Pagan (STScI)/flickr.com; page 15: ©X-ray: NASA/CXC; Optical: NASA/STScI/nasa.gov; page 19: ©Javier Zayas Photography/Getty Images; page 20: ©ESA/Webb, NASA and CSA, A. Martel./flickr.com; page 25: ©MARK GARLICK/SCIENCE PHOTO LIBRARY/Getty Images; page 26: ©NASA, ESA, CSA, Tommaso Treu (UCLA)/flickr.com; page 29: ©NASA, ESA, R. Windhorst, S. Cohen, M. Mechtley, and M. Rutkowski (Arizona State University, Tempe), R. O'Connell (University of Virginia), P. McCarthy (Carnegie Observatories), N. Hathi (University of California, Riverside), R. Ryan (University of California, Davis), H. Yan (Ohio State University), and A. Koekemoer (Space Telescope Science Institute)/nasa.gov

Cherry Lake Press is an imprint of Cherry Lake Publishing Group.

Library of Congress Cataloging-in-Publication Data
Library of Congress Cataloging-in-Publication Data has been filed and is available at catalog.loc.gov

ISBN 9781668938348 Lib.

Cherry Lake Publishing Group would like to acknowledge the work of the Partnership for 21st Century Learning, a Network of Battelle for Kids. Please visit Battelle for Kids online for more information.

Note from publisher: Websites change regularly, and their future contents are outside of our control. Supervise children when conducting any recommended online searches for extended learning opportunities.

Printed in the United States of America

Mari Bolte is an author and editor of children's books in every subject imaginable. She hopes the next generation sets their sights on the sky and beyond. Never stop the love of learning!

CONTENTS

CHAPTER 1

Look into the Deep

Look up at the sky. There are billions of stars out there. From Earth, they look like shining white dots on a dark sky. The light from each star travels great distances to get to us. Our Sun is a star. It's the closest star to us. But it's still between 91.3 and 94.4 million miles (147 and 152 million kilometers) away. Light travels 186,000 miles (300,000 km) per second. The Sun's light takes around 500 seconds to reach us.

The stars we can see in the night sky aren't part of our solar system. Polaris, also known as the North Star, is an example. It is a bright star in our sky, but it is 323 **light-years** away. We actually see Polaris as it appeared 323 years ago. When we look at stars, we look back in time.

Polaris is nearly directly above Earth's axis. That means that it never appears to move in the sky, even as Earth spins. Anyone in the top half of the planet can follow the star and travel directly north.

Telescopes let us look even farther. Their cameras see light that is invisible to the human eye. They can take pictures of the sky using long exposure times. This lets them see faint, faraway objects. The *James Webb Space Telescope* can take deep-field images. Deep-field images are pictures taken over many hours. They capture ancient light from billions of years ago.

Camera Facts

The *James Webb*'s cameras can COLLECT LIGHT INFORMATION for hours, or even days. This allows it to find faint, small, or very faraway objects.

With stationary cameras on Earth, long **exposure** times capture STAR TRAILS. The trails show the motion of the stars and Earth's rotation.

The human eye sends information to the brain in 1/15TH OF A SECOND. A cell phone's camera can have exposure times as fast as 1/8,000th of a second or as slow as 20 or 30 seconds.

CHAPTER 2

Webb's First Deep Field

SMACS 0723 is a faraway **galaxy cluster**. It was one of the first things the *James Webb Space Telescope* focused on when its mission began in 2022. This galaxy cluster is in an area of space that is deep and distant. The stars, planets, and galaxies in this direction are billions of light-years away. *Webb* made seeing those objects in much greater detail possible.

Webb's main tool is called the Near-**Infrared** Camera (NIRCam). Objects with bright lights can block dimmer objects nearby. NIRCam can see past those bright lights. It can also focus clearly on objects no matter how far away they are. The photo NIRCam sent back of SMACS 0723 showed thousands of galaxies in one shot. Everything was sharp and clear. There were even tiny details and different

The Volans constellation is also known as the Flying Fish. It flies through the sky alongside a ship of stars.

colors in the image. It was *Webb*'s first deep-field image.

If you ever get the chance to visit the Southern Hemisphere, you can look toward SMACS 0723. In the spring, find the constellation Volans in the sky. It is near the very bright star Miaplacidus. Point a finger in its direction. Pretend there's a laser coming out of your fingertip. The photo *Webb* took would fit inside that laser. There are thousands of galaxies in the image.

NIRCam is just one of four of *Webb*'s high-tech gadgets. The telescope's other instruments, or scientific tools, give scientists a different view of the same thing. Some instruments are better at looking at certain types of objects. An instrument may even have multiple observing modes.

Webb took 12.5 hours to collect this deep field. It used different **wavelengths**. It shows things as they EXISTED 13.1 BILLION YEARS AGO.

Red objects are surrounded by space dust. Green are rich in chemicals. Blue are galaxies with stars but very little SPACE DUST.

SMACS 0723 Facts

Closer objects are BRIGHT AND CLEAR. Longer-length observations reveal fainter objects that have never been seen before.

Webb Instruments

A guide to some of *Webb*'s most high-tech gadgets:

Near-Infrared Camera (NIRCam)

- clear focus on objects near and far
- can find dimmer objects near bright objects

Near-Infrared Spectrograph (NIRSpec)

- no camera
- measures the brightness of individual objects

Mid-Infrared Instrument (MIRI)

- takes images that show space dust
- shows scientists where stars are being formed
- helps scientists find **exoplanets**

Near-Infrared Imager and Slitless Spectrograph (NIRISS)

- highest-quality images of bright objects

Fine Guidance Sensor (FGS)

- stabilizes *Webb*
- keeps *Webb* pointing in the right direction (works as the navigator)

The arrow in the image points to Earendel. The entire galaxy is known as the Sunrise Arc.

A NEW PERSPECTIVE

The *Hubble Space Telescope* has been taking photos of space since 1990. *Webb*'s and *Hubble*'s cameras "see" in different wavelengths. They can take pictures of the same things and send back very different images.

The space telescopes have been placed at different places in the solar system. *Hubble* orbits Earth. It's 332 miles (534 km) away from us. *Webb* is more than 1 million miles (1.6 million km) away. It orbits the Sun.

Hubble helped us see the farthest-away star we have ever seen. It is called Earendel. *Hubble* was able to photograph it in March 2022. The light came from 12.9 billion light-years away. But the universe has expanded since then. So this distant star is now 28 billion light-years from Earth. *Webb* took its own picture of Earendel in August 2023, allowing scientists to explore this faraway star from a whole new perspective.

CHAPTER 3

Pandora's Cluster

Webb has shown us that we're just a tiny speck in an enormous, endless sky. Its **panoramic** picture of Pandora's Cluster makes that even more clear. It shows more than 50,000 sources of near-infrared light. Near-infrared cameras can see through super-cold space dust. That dust can hide stars, asteroids, and failed stars called brown dwarfs.

Pandora's Cluster is about 4 billion light-years away. It is also known as Abell 2744. It is a huge cluster made up of at least four smaller galaxy clusters. They spent 350 million years crashing into each other. *Hubble* first showed us the area in 2011. But its cameras could only study Pandora's central core. *Webb*'s infrared imagery was able to capture three of the clusters in greater detail.

Pandora's Cluster is located near the center of this image. *Webb*'s cameras were able to pick up objects in the cluster that were 10 to 20 times fainter than any galaxies seen before.

A galaxy cluster on its own is one of the most massive objects in space, with the strongest gravity. Pandora's galaxy clusters have formed a megacluster. Their combined **mass** and gravity are enormous. It is so strong, it bends light around it. This warped area acts like a magnifying glass. Objects behind it appear bigger and brighter than normal. Without this effect, *Webb* would not be able to look so deep into space—or so far back into time.

NIRCam shot images of Pandora's Cluster using 4- to 6-hour-long exposures. In total, around 30 HOURS OF OBSERVING TIME was recorded.

Pandora's Cluster Facts

Some distant galaxies are red and look bent. This is due to the MAGNIFYING EFFECT, CALLED GRAVITATIONAL LENSING. Faint arc-shaped lines are other distant galaxies.

Pandora was a character in Greek mythology. She opened a box, releasing things like sickness, death, and evil into the world. PANDORA'S CLUSTER was named after her because of the different and strange things that were released during the collision of galaxies.

CHAPTER 4

A Fossil in Space

Fossils can tell scientists about what life was like on Earth millions of years ago. But there are fossils in space, too. **Galactic fossils** are galaxies that are billions of years old. As the universe expands, the light from these galaxies stretches into infrared light.

Scientists can learn more about the Milky Way by comparing the images of fossils to known objects in our galaxy. They can look at the fossils and learn how old they are. They can figure out how big and how far away they are. Finding more fossils means being able to shape a clearer picture of our own galaxy.

On May 22, 2022, scientists were making sure everything on *Webb*'s NIRCam was working correctly. They wanted to see how well the camera could find galactic fossils. NIRCam

Hercules is part of one of the brightest star clusters in the sky. It can be seen from Earth with just binoculars.

was aimed at the constellation Hercules. This can be seen in the northern sky. What the telescope sent back was the most detailed shot of galactic fossils ever taken.

Fossil Facts

The EIGHT-POINTED spiked objects in the image are stars.

Small SPIRAL GALAXIES can be seen up close. Others are too small to see in great detail. They look like smudges or pinpricks.

Scientists compare images of GALACTIC "FOSSILS" to closer, newer galaxies to learn more about how they change over time.

LEDA 2046648 is the large spiral galaxy in the top-center of the image on the previous spread. It is around a billion light-years away. That means the light we see in the image is old. It is as old as the very first single-celled organisms on Earth. This is what makes LEDA 2046648 a galactic fossil. LEDA 2046648 is also very similar to the Milky Way.

Above LEDA 2046648 is a smaller spiral galaxy. It is about one-quarter the size. Both have glowing cores. Pale pink arms spiral from the centers. Around 60 percent of all galaxies are spiral galaxies. This means that most of the stars in the universe are part of spiral galaxies. But 6 billion years ago, more than half of those known spiral galaxies were "peculiar." This means they were unusually sized. Or they had interesting shapes or chemical makeups. Over time, they collided or merged with other galaxies. They became spirals.

How galaxies form and grow is valuable information. The Milky Way has avoided extreme collisions so far. But our nearest neighbor, the Andromeda Galaxy, has not. More than 200 million years ago, it collided with a neighboring dwarf galaxy. Scientists are trying to figure out why the Milky Way is still mostly untouched.

Forced Perspective

When you look into outer space, everything seems impossibly far away. But some things are much, much farther away than others. Imagine we could travel at light speed. How long would it take to get there?

	Distance from Earth	Travel Time
Moon	238,855 miles (384,400 km)	1.25 seconds
Sun	93.1 million miles (149.8 km)	8 minutes
Pluto	3.2 billion miles (5.1 billion km)	5.5 hours
Orion Nebula	1,344 light-years	1,344 years
Andromeda Galaxy	2.5 million light-years	2.5 million years
Earendel	over 28 billion light-years	over 28 billion years

CHAPTER 5

The Most Distant Starlight

When and how the first stars were born remains a mystery. Scientists have always had ideas, though. Most believe the universe was formed during the **Big Bang**. That's when the expansion of the universe began. This was 13.8 billion years ago. Scientists thought that the first stars started to form 100 million years after that event. Small clouds of gas and clusters of stars eventually mixed. They formed early galaxies. These galaxies were simple and rare. Then, scientists thought, the first real galaxies took another billion years to appear.

But what the *James Webb* found in November 2022 shocked scientists. It upended what they thought they knew. *Webb* found two early galaxies in Pandora's Cluster.

Although we will never see the moment of the Big Bang for ourselves, artists have tried to recreate it in a way that is easy to understand.

They were shaped like spheres or disks. Their light was very bright. And they were as complex as the Milky Way. These complex galaxies, not just simple galaxies, started to form 100 million years after the Big Bang.

That's 1 billion years earlier than what was previously believed. This discovery sent ripples through the scientific community. Some **skeptics** of the Big Bang saw this image as evidence that the moment never happened. Under the Big Bang model, these galaxies should not exist. They are too big, too old, and too well-formed. Was the Big Bang **theory** broken into bits?

Ancient Galaxy Facts

1

As the ANCIENT GALAXIES expand and age, their light moves to longer, redder (infrared) wavelengths. Capturing infrared light is one of *Webb*'s specialties.

1   z~10.5

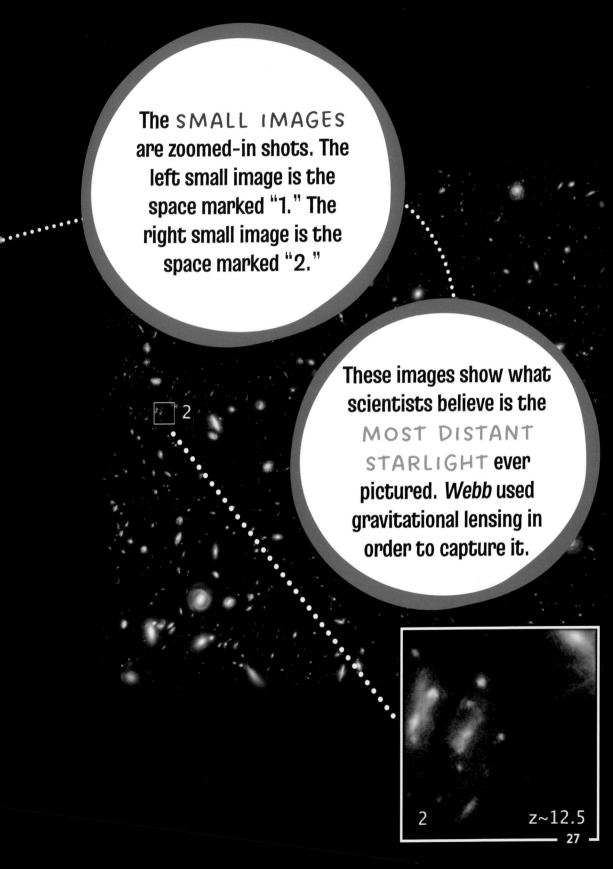

The SMALL IMAGES are zoomed-in shots. The left small image is the space marked "1." The right small image is the space marked "2."

These images show what scientists believe is the MOST DISTANT STARLIGHT ever pictured. *Webb* used gravitational lensing in order to capture it.

2

2   z~12.5

The *James Webb Space Telescope* backed up its discovery in April 2023. It looked back 13.4 billion years. And it saw hundreds of thousands of complex galaxies. They were full of stars. One of the galaxies was making stars as fast as the Milky Way, even though it was 100 times less massive.

Scientists concluded that *Webb*'s images did not disprove the Big Bang theory. But they did disprove some **models** of the early universe. Researchers had expected to find galaxies as old as Pandora's Cluster. The big surprise was that they were so well-structured and numerous. Scientists had been wrong about early galaxies. *Webb* showed that they grew faster than scientists thought. New models are now being made from this information. But the Big Bang theory still holds—at least for now.

Science is about always learning and discovering. New evidence is being gathered. Theories are being tested. Models are being adjusted. *Webb* is giving us a greater understanding of our universe and beyond. Someday, scientists hope it will show them the moment when stars and galaxies first burst into being. But even after that happens, *Webb*'s work won't be done. With billions of unknowns in the sky, there is always more to discover.

NIRCam and NIRSpec worked together to discover the types of gases and stars inside previously studied fields of space.

A DEEPER DEEP FIELD

Webb's tools can work independently. They can also work together! NIRCam's and NIRSpec's teams collaborated. Their joint program is called the *JWST* Advanced Deep **Extragalactic** Survey (JADES). The mission first focused on *Hubble*'s Ultra Deep Field. This area of space revealed 10,000 galaxies to *Hubble*'s cameras. The cameras were able to look at a narrow slice of the stars and galaxies. The deeper a space telescope looks into space, the older the galaxies are.

JADES was able to take an even more detailed look. Nearly 100,000 galaxies were captured. The images taken by JADES will be compared to those taken by *Hubble* and other earlier space telescopes.

Activity

Connect to STEAM: Science

In 1977, *Voyagers I* and *II* carried golden records into space. They were time capsules! Each record contained sounds and images meant to tell aliens about Earth. A lot of time has passed since 1977, and Earth has changed. Now, thanks to the *James Webb Space Telescope*, we know that there are many unexplored planets that could support alien life! What if you could send a time capsule to outer space? Make a list of everything you would include in your time capsule.

MATERIALS NEEDED

- paper
- writing utensils

1. Think about who your time capsule is for. Would you want it to be discovered by a scientist? Another kid? Or even the leader of an alien species?

2. What would you like them to know about life today? News articles, photographs, and pieces of technology would give them a view of our culture. Toys, journals, letters, and pictures are other things to include.

3. Tell the aliens what you like to eat, play, or do. Describe those activities as if you're explaining them to someone who doesn't know what they are. Be sure to include rules and other details so they can try it themselves!

4. Add things from holidays or special occasions. Show them how you celebrate!

5. Draw a picture of your neighborhood, your car, or your favorite video game. Think of something that would be very surprising to see!

Find Out More

Books

Bolte, Mari. *Space Mysteries*. Ann Arbor, MI: Cherry Lake Publishing Group, 2023.

Collins, Ailynn. *Investigating the Milky Way and Other Galaxies with Velma*. North Mankato, MN: Capstone Press, 2024.

Golusky, Jackie. *Weird Space*. Minneapolis: Lerner Publications, 2024.

Schaefer, Lola M. *Explore Telescopes*. Minneapolis: Lerner Publications, 2023.

Online Resources to Search with an Adult

Ariane Group: Find Out About the Launch of the *James Webb Telescope*

Ducksters: Physics for Kids

NASA: *James Webb Space Telescope*

Webb Space Telescope: How Does *Webb* See Back in Time?

Glossary

Big Bang (BIG BAYNG) an explosion that scientists believe started the formation of the universe

exoplanets (EK-soh-pla-nuhtz) planets outside our solar system

exposure (ek-SPOH-zhuhr) the amount of light that reaches a camera; over time, that light is turned into information we can see

exposure times (ik-SPOH-zhuhr TIEMZ) lengths of time that cameras collect light while taking pictures

extragalactic (ek-struh-guh-LAK-tik) outside the Milky Way Galaxy

galactic fossils (guh-LAK-tik FAH-suhlz) ancient galaxies

galaxy cluster (GA-luhk-see KLUH-stuhr) a collection of hundreds or thousands of galaxies

infrared (in-fruh-RED) invisible light from beyond the red end of the visible light spectrum

light-years (LYTE-YEERZ) units of distance equal to how far light travels in 1 year—6 trillion miles (9.6 trillion km)

mass (MAS) how much material an object contains, giving it weight when influenced by gravity

models (MAH-duhlz) representations, such as images, equations, or computer programs, used as a tool to understand or predict complex ideas

panoramic (pa-nuh-RA-mik) having a wide view

skeptics (SKEP-tiks) people who doubt a certain statement is true

theory (THEE-uh-ree) a scientifically accepted explanation of current observations and understandings about an aspect of the natural world

wavelengths (WAYV-lengths) measurements between one wave to another as energy flows through space in a wavelike pattern

Index